Cab Story
A play by Dorit Kedar

featuring the Seven Sins *series of paintings*

✶
The Center of Inter-religious Peace, Tel Aviv

THE CENTER OF INTER-RELIGIOUS PEACE
Tel Aviv, Israel

The Center of Inter-religious Peace
15 Oley Ha'Gardom St., Tel Aviv 6971523 ISRAEL

http://doritkedar.wordpress.com/

Cab Story, A Play
Seven Sins series of paintings

Original Hebrew title: *Sipurei moniyot*
Translation, editing, and introduction: Tzach Ben Josef
Original typing (in Hebrew): Sharon Yafe
Original editing for theater production (in Hebrew): Charlie Buzaglo

Layout and design: Tzach Ben Josef
Cover design and digital mastering: Gall Orian
Photography: Revital Topiol
Paintings: Dorit Kedar
Cover: *Fantasy*, detail, see page 38

© Dorit Kedar, The Center of Inter-religious Peace, 2014

This publication is in copyright. No part of this publication may be reproduced, stored in retrieval system, or transmitted, in any form or by any means, without the permission in writing of the Center of Inter-religious Peace, or as expressly permitted by law, or under terms agreed with the appropriate reprographics rights organizations.

ISBN 9789659214723

Printed by CreateSpace

Cab Story

Translation and Introduction by
Tzach Ben Josef

Contents

Introduction   *7*

The Play   *7*

About the author *69*

Introduction

Look at it this way. A man takes a job, you know? And that job–I mean, like, that–that becomes what he is. You know, like–you do a thing and that's what you are.
> – *Wizard*, Taxi Driver *(1976)*

Wizard was probably right when he uttered these words to Robert De Niro's character Travis in *Taxi Driver*. Insanity, colorfulness, sensuality and misery– all pass through Travis' taxicab and are the lifeline of the characters that pass in and out of his life; violence, lechery, sex, and despair govern their lives. The play *Cab Story* elicits a similar impression. Although the play is situated in a different urban setting and breaks with the film's pessimistic mindset, its varied characters share basic urges and passions with those of the film's; these very basic and turbulent urges that all people share gush over, sometimes at the most unexpected moment, and are constantly being restrained and tabooed by society.

*Cab Story * Dorit Kedar*

Taxi drivers that come across these human phenomena and try to make sense of them are at the heart of this play. If, much like Wizard's claims, the taxi driver's type of work makes up the legend to the map that charts his being, its symbols–the basic urges of the types that get on and off of his cab, then their map is not made up any differently.

These urges come across in the lives of the driver characters in Dorit Kedar's play written during the 1990's. With no driving license the playwright had to spend an ample amount of time intensively consorting with the driver. The latter, confined just as much as the passenger to the same time and space, pours his heart out to her, and the former, out of exceptional aptitude of a good listener, finds herself on the seat of a therapist who specializes in cab drivers. In each of the fourteen segments that make up the play different drivers open up to the passenger. Each one starts off a tragi-comic voyage, starting with the driver's basic function as a vehicle transporting the passenger from A to B and gearing towards unfolding stories of human conditions and of most basic of urges.

Beginning in May 2002, the play was performed over a year and a half at the "Simta" Theater in Jaffa. The one-woman show preformed by the playwright was directed by Irit Frank. With the least of theatrical performance conditions, the utmost of everyday occurrences were brought to the fore. The endless variety of human characteristics of the characters in the drivers' tales was delivered on an empty stage through movement, mimicry, and voice.

Cab Story * Dorit Kedar

The *Seven Sins* series of paintings, executed by the playwright as well, acted as the sole "scenery," a different picture shown for each segment. An interpretation of the Seven Deadly Sins, each work-executed in oil on wood, and measuring 39 by 27 inches-relates to a different nature of each segment. The artist fabricated a multidisciplinary event, interweaving text, image, movement, and voice into a web, much like the tangled one in which every person desperately tries to ensnare his/her darkest of passions every day, only to have them seep through the holes.

The English version has not been put to the stage and is brought to the attention of the international reader for the first time. The cab rides took place in Israel and the dialogue between the characters relies on idioms in the Hebrew language. Nevertheless, the language has been more colloquially adapted without displacing the setting. Although knowledge of Israeli cultural attitudes and differences would benefit the reader in understanding the type of the Israeli cab driver, the one lacking it will not be at a disadvantage: the play, after all, reflects not on the lives of taxicab drivers in particular, but on that which is common to all people, everywhere. Proper names have not been changed. Ancillary information has been provided where needed.

The Play

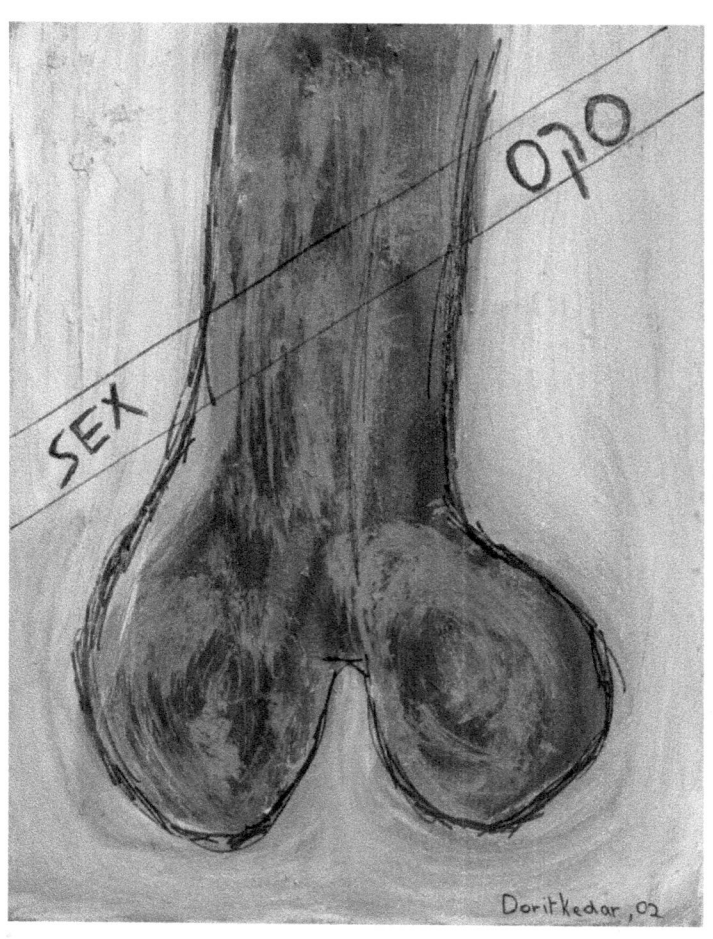

*Cab Story * Dorit Kedar*

From Ramat HaChaiil to "Yefet" Gallery in Jaffa

DRIVER: Hija!* Haven't seen you for a long time!
*(term of endearment; from Spanish: hijo–son; hija–daughter)

THE PASSENGER: And I haven't seen you, how are you? What about that nurse from the hospital? Is she still relevant?

DRIVER: What can I tell you, hija, with and without her, we're having problems, you know. I went to America to see the grandchildren. Here, I'll show you a picture. What do you say? Sweet as sugar he is, huh? And she didn't want to come along. She also has grandchildren and besides, she and my daughter–it's only so so… you know. Hija, don't ask! I met this young one, from Thailand, a real beauty–a piece of candy she is, I tell you! What a life! Something else! A real treat. Yeah, a big treat. And you, how have you been doing?

THE PASSENGER: I'm fine, hijo, went and got my head opened a year ago.

DRIVER: What do you mean your head?

THE PASSENGER: A tumor.

DRIVER: No!

THE PASSENGER: Yes!

DRIVER: Let me tell you something. I had a tumor on my spine. It was cancer. Had this operation, radiations, what not. This Thai woman of mine- such health. Today is Friday. Excuse me for telling you this, but I'm already in a rush to get home. You don't know what it's like to have a girl from Thailand. What will I tell you, you look like a smart lady. Nothing beats a girl from Thailand, a dream, pure heaven. I come home and she baths me, feeds me, more and more food, and then we're off to bed. She's petite, don't mind me telling you, huh, but I put a pillow under her so her ass's higher and then, pure heaven!

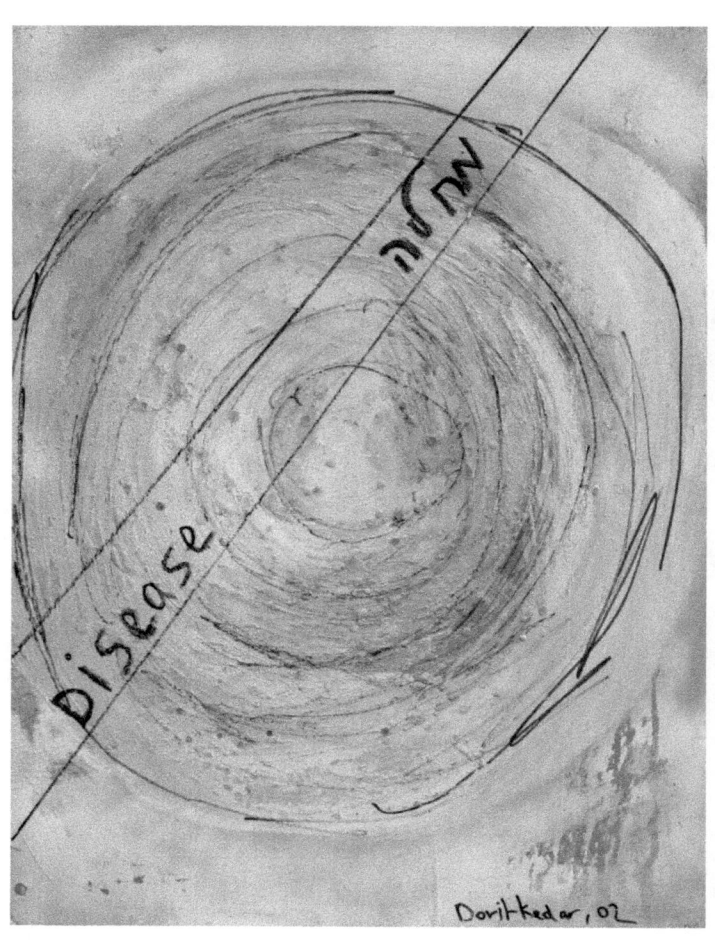

Cab Story * Dorit Kedar

From Arlozorov train station home, at night

DRIVER: Watch it! Sorry for braking so hard. That guy was looking for a hooker and cut me off. This whole roundabout is teeming with hookers. What do you think of hookers, yourself?

THE PASSENGER: Poor souls, nothing but hardship.

DRIVER: And even if I offered you, say, 14,000?

THE PASSENGER: In Shekels or Dollars? There are few people who cannot be bought.

DRIVER: I don't know what kind of childhood you had, but if you knew who my father had been, you'd open the window and climb right out.

THE PASSENGER: You are not your father, though. You're not a felon, are you?

DRIVER: True, true, god forbid. But in the fifties my father was a known felon. We grew up in this shed with no indoor toilet. At night, you had to go out into the dark, with these thorns sticking you. There were nine of us. My sisters were afraid of the dark and they used to wet their bed. Only my father used a night pot and he used to make them throw it out and if they refused, he gave them spoons and ordered them to eat it. Since he's dead, I still can't believe it. I'm afraid he would rise from his grave. One of my brothers–a lunatic–our father hit him with a board with nails sticking out of it and during his funeral, they asked him to ask our father's forgiveness and he had the guts to say to that corpse laying there, "you should be the one asking for forgiveness." We were scared out of our wits of him. Our mother was afraid as well, poor thing, he ran her to an early grave. We owe her everything. None of us is a felon, we are all good working men. Once my father set the house on fire and told my mother he'd burn her and the children. She screamed and one of our neighbors, a real thug from Bat Yam, came into the burning house and yelled for us to come out, but we were so scared stiff that we did not budge. And that guy cursed at us, screaming, and kicking us out the door with his feet. Then he turned on dad and told him to burn himself alive, but he didn't. I'm sorry, could you read this out to me, it's for a doctor's appointment, something about my health, I'm sick. I'm going through a tough examination tomorrow. I swear, I have got to stop smoking. I'm sorry, could you read this for me?

THE PASSENGER: It says you should have this test done and you really should. I wish you all the best. It reeks of cigarettes here. With your permission, I'm rolling the window down. Excuse me, are you lighting a cigarette? I would really rather if you didn't!

DRIVER: But you say it reeks here anyway, so what is the difference?

THE PASSENGER: Because it'll stink even more and I've had just about enough. You're looking at me through the rear-view mirror, bubba. My lungs are gone anyhow, so don't get mad. When I was younger I accidently drank some gasoline and my mother didn't know not to move someone who had and she grabbed me by the feet and tossed me around, so the gasoline went straight to my lungs.

DRIVER: Your lungs can't be any worse than mine. Do you know for how long I have smoked? I can't feel my arm, that's how long. It goes numb at the top. And besides, those tests are for my stomach. I also bleed from my gums, all on account of these cigarettes.

THE PASSENGER: So maybe you should quit? A friend of mine died of a gangrene and it could happen to you, too.

DRIVER: I'm a mess. Honestly, I'm quitting!

THE PASSENGER: How many cigarettes have you got left there?

DRIVER: Two. Two last ones and that's that.

THE PASSENGER: No, no, these are the last ones, these you throw away.

DRIVER: Throw?

THE PASSENGER: Would you like me to do it for you? I'm getting off and there's a large trash bin right ahead. You could watch as I ceremoniously chuck them, couldn't you?

DRIVER: Go ahead, go ahead. Sweetheart, all the best to you, maybe you'd be the one to turn me around!

Cab Story * Dorit Kedar

From Ramat Ha'Chaiil to Tel Aviv center

DRIVER: Present company excluded, but you should know it's like a garbage truck in here. I only get trash here. They think they can buy you, like you're some sort of slave of theirs– "go," "stop," no "excuse me," no "thank you," they smoke, leave their shit in here. One lady came from the market with some herring. I told her, "easy now, I don't pick up groceries." She's all like "nothing to worry about." She sits down and looking to see if the fish are fresh, dumps them all over my carpeting and upholstery, and all day I stunk like a herring. You can't get it out, you know. Nothing helps. I had to sell the cab. Sure the poor guy didn't know that in a while the car's gonna stink up like a dead pile of fish, after the deodorizer fades. But what could I do? Swim with the fish?

THE PASSENGER: In a moment I'll put some perfume on and it'll smell great in here.

DRIVER: Say, could you drizzle some on the seats?

THE PASSENGER: Seriously? This is expensive. A little aroma for ambience will suffice.

DRIVER: I have a regular that sprays the seats and the vents. As soon as she gets off, I roll down the windows.

THE PASSENGER: Then why don't you tell her to stop?

DRIVER: I do, but it doesn't help. She's a senior bank employee. A good woman. Never married. Poor thing, at fifty, takes care of her mom, her brother. She can call a cab to Bat Yam, hand out a few copies of some women's magazine and come back. She's innocent, stayed single, the poor thing.

THE PASSENGER: Not all single women are a "poor thing." I, for one, am single.

DRIVER: Of your own choice, no doubt. She, on the other hand, is anxious to get married.

THE PASSENGER: So?

DRIVER: Ahh, with her mother and brother, who will take her and besides, all those people taking advantage of others who are so innocent. For those animals it's fair game!

Cab Story ∗ *Dorit Kedar*

From Ramat Ha'Chaiil to Tel Aviv center

DRIVER: Now you see me a cabby and with this old piece of metal, but, boy, was I once rich with so many friends. We drank, we ate, had a ball, so many friends. One bankruptcy and they all were gone. No one to help. No one to come over. One day, and you're out of friends.

THE PASSENGER: It seems that your choice of friends wasn't very good. You should have picked them by character, not by what you were doing together, eating and drinking…

DRIVER: Listen, lady, I thank god I went bankrupt. It was a blessing in disguise. You are so right to be saying what you are. I have other friends around me now, totally different. Good and honest, and straight like an arrow.

THE PASSENGER: What time do you get off today?

DRIVER: Look, you can't work 12 hours straight. You remember that other guy who picked you up instead of me? He had it all. Got married and got a house and his own cab. But he didn't get it that the cash he got wasn't just his, some goes to the government, for repairs, insurance, what not, that fool just didn't get it. Sold his house, then his cab, then his plates, and all he had left was a bad back.

THE PASSENGER: It's a good thing you have these blinders, they give such a nice shadow.

DRIVER: You have no idea what a hassle these things are. All the clients get in and ask why they're there for, ask me if I drive VIPs around all day. Some even ask, "What? Do I look like the president to you?"

THE PASSENGER: And how do you respond?

DRIVER: How can I? I ask them back, "what? You're not?" Am I supposed to go at it with them…? This guy gets in the other day, sits in the seat next to me, moves my mirror, puts his hands on his head and goes like this, this. What do you say to that? And this lady gets in with her two kids and all the while she has her head out the window and the kids are screaming and crying and touching all the knobs, and she has her head out, can't hear a thing, can't see a thing, and on top of that even brings this small dog in with her!

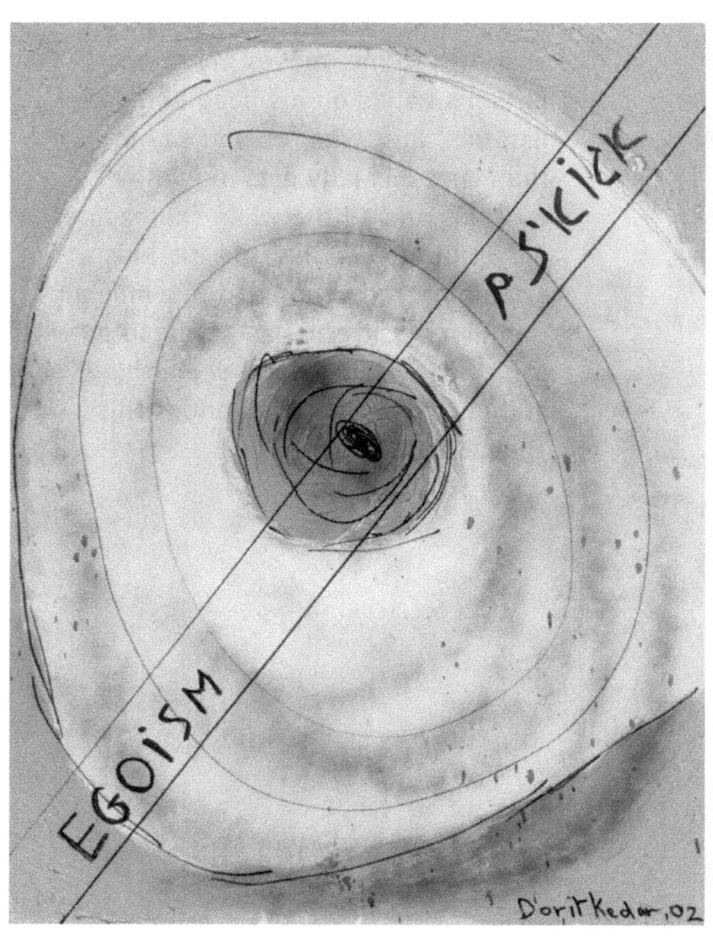

*Cab Story * Dorit Kedar*

From Ramat Ha'Chaiil to the Tel Aviv Performing Arts Center

THE PASSENGER: I've been waiting longer than 20 minutes for you and now I'll miss the start of the opera.

DRIVER: I'm sorry, but let me tell you that I was held at the airport for 8 hours and I kept calling Sofia. I'm Bulgarian and have a girl in Sofia. I met her the last time I was there. We traveled all over Bulgaria, stayed at fancy hotels, too. It's real cheap there. I was held at the airport. Something was wrong. I called and I called her and my calling card ran out so I went back home. A few days later I wanted to go to Bulgaria to see her, but they told me she was in the hospital, can't move a thing. She was clearing some shelves in a closet for me, and fell down and broke her hip. Well, I waited for a while and planned my trip and you wouldn't believe it, I got a hernia.

I asked the state to bring her over, but they don't let gentiles come over here that easily. What can I do? Now I got an Israeli girl. She lives in, but I made her sign this thing that it's my house, not hers. She's upset, what can I do?

THE PASSENGER: You have a new car, congratulations.

DRIVER: I'm also new.

THE PASSENGER: I can see that. Did you get a look at that guy? Bleached hair, tattoos, wild, high boots, walks like a macho man, oozing with violence.

DRIVER: It's all on the account of the pot, lady. The pot. Didn't you read last week in the paper, on page 26, that it screws with your head and gives you mood swings? Something like that bipolar thing. Pot messes with the brain cells.

THE PASSENGER: How would you know?

DRIVER: Been married 5 years to a pothead of 20 years now.

THE PASSENGER: And you knew this going into that marriage?

DRIVER: I knew and I didn't. God loves me, though. I got divorced 3 months back. You know how many fertility treatments we've had? And nothing, all because of that pot. She also works at the station. Airhead! Hits on the dispatcher to set her up with lots of fares. Say, can't I run my hand down your body? Boy, would I love to! Why not? Do you mind if I came over to your place? You'll see, it'll be a real treat, come on.

THE PASSENGER: Look, bubba, with all the offers I've got from cab drivers, I could open a brothel on wheels, but it's tough changing vocation at my age. Tell me, now seriously, what's with you, being in heat like that? What's wrong?

DRIVER: I'm afraid of dying. Sweetheart, you see this beard? Last time I picked you up I didn't have it. My brother died a week back, high blood pressure, I have it also.

THE PASSENGER: You should see someone about that.

DRIVER: I do, I do. They gave me anti-depressants.

THE PASSENGER: And you've been taking them?

DRIVER: Sure, but it doesn't help. So what do you say, sweetheart, no go?

Cab Story * *Dorit Kedar*

Sitting at the Arlozorov station at night

DRIVER: It's a good thing you're sitting close to me, it's late and there aren't any cabs or buses running now and the place if full of hookers.

THE PASSENGER: How much is it?

DRIVER: We'll figure something out.

THE PASSENGER: I gave this woman a ride to Bat Yam once and on the way back someone flagged me down. A young girl, wanted to Jaffa, but had only 5 shekels. But since it was on my way anyway, I told her to get in. In the middle of the ride I can feel her hand between my legs. So startled, I flinched and told her, "get out!" I opened the door to kick her out, she got out and started to yell, "you're not a real man!" and to curse, too. What an ordeal. They'd end up saying I raped her, for sure. Who's gonna believe she stuck her hand down my crotch. So I slammed the door and scrammed right outta there.

THE PASSENGER: Maybe she was a hooker?

DRIVER: Not on your life! If she was, then she'd take 50, 70 shekels, she was an amateur.

THE PASSENGER: 50, 70 shekels? That cheap?

DRIVER: What do you think? There's so many of them, strong competition, not all of them charge so little. You have these fancy call girls, 300 bucks a night, and she comes to your hotel, looking all sleek. You have these other girls for 200 dollars a pop, they invite over to an apartment.

THE PASSENGER: Where do they live?

DRIVER: There's one in each building in Tel Aviv, and who knows what blows in and out of there. You're not bad looking, you know?

THE PASSENGER: Thank you.

DRIVER: For real!

THE PASSENGER: I take it, "for real."

*Cab Story * Dorit Kedar*

DRIVER: Better a real woman than a 25-year-old girl. A couple of days ago, I took this mother, a daughter of 25 and a little girl. The 25-year-old sat next to me. I saw her giving me these looks and it was nice and we laughed and stuff. At the end of the ride, after her mother gets off, she slips me her number. You probably think I called her? I did not! Let me tell you something that happened to a buddy of mine, a father of five, never lied eyes on another girl's bra but his wife's, he didn't. One day he was called for a job in Ramla. He goes over there and this lady opens the door with a see-through gown. He starts working on the pipes and she starts running her hand over his head, and he's only human, so he went for it! And what do you think happened?

THE PASSENGER: What?

DRIVER: She goes, "either you give me a grand now or I call the cops and tell them you raped me." He didn't give her anything. Today he's in prison five years already. His wife divorced him, his life's in shambles. So, what do you say about grabbing a cup of coffee? No, not in some noisy place, I'm sleek. We'll go to the Hilton, it's quiet there. No? Your loss!

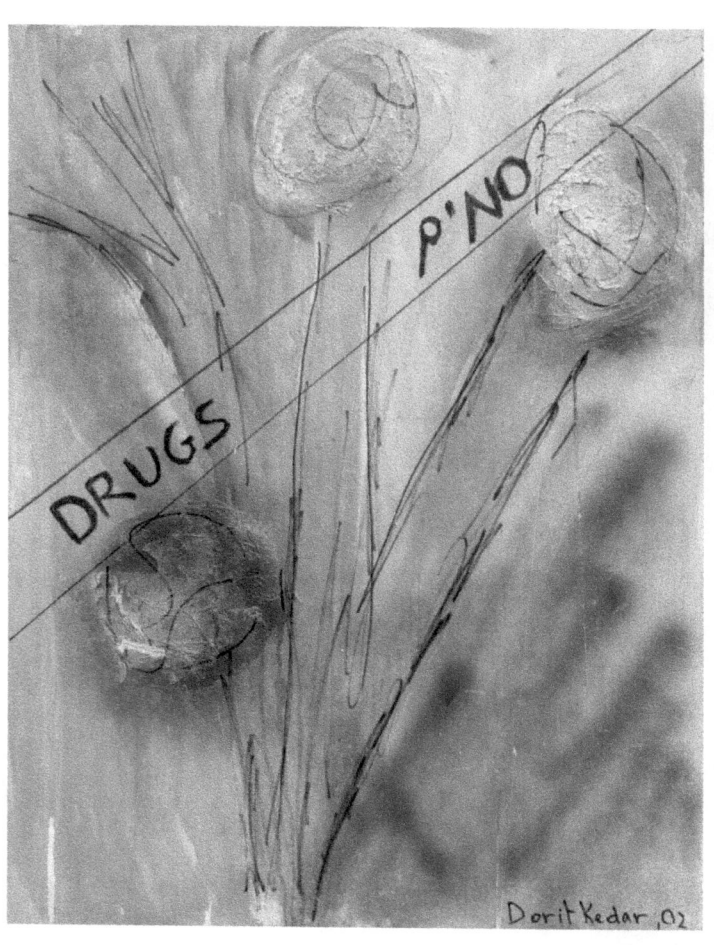

Cab Story * Dorit Kedar

From "Yefet" Gallery in Jaffa to "Dizzingoff Center"

THE PASSENGER: In a cab before there was a junky. After he got out, I asked to Dizzingoff Center, but the driver refused. Another one came, and two hookers, I believe it was, got out. And that driver too refused to take me. What do you think was going on there?

DRIVER: Look, there's this line of cabs that specializes in hookers and junkies. They take them from here, Jaffa, in a snap to Lod and back for 150 shekels. Good money, off the meter, no papers. But they'll pay dearly one day. 'Scuse my French, but the shit holes they take them to, you could get murdered, and even if you scream, for help, no one will come. You'll drive around junkies for ten years, one of them will end up sticking a knife in you. Say, you'd let just about anyone into your home?

THE PASSENGER: No.

DRIVER: Then why should I let into my cab? Junkies, drunks—I know all their tricks. They don't say "Lod," but "Ramla, Ramla." Then you get there and they say to make a right at the tracks and wait, then I let them off. No, no, I'm not scared, I carry a piece. One time this drunk got in and threatened that he'll complain about me to the DMV, wanted my number and all, the piece of shit! These drunks never pay, they fall asleep. You know what a sleeping drunk is like? Try waking one up, sleeps like a log, doesn't want to get out. "Get off, don't pay!" I tell him, and he doesn't pay or get out. Tells me to leave him alone, it's his bed, his house, and I can go screw myself. So I let them off from the start. No, no, not really, I drop them off somewhere safe in the street but never pick them up again. That'll be 25 shekels.

THE PASSENGER: No, no, put the meter on.

DRIVER: You see? That's why they don't let you in—you've got papers written all over you.

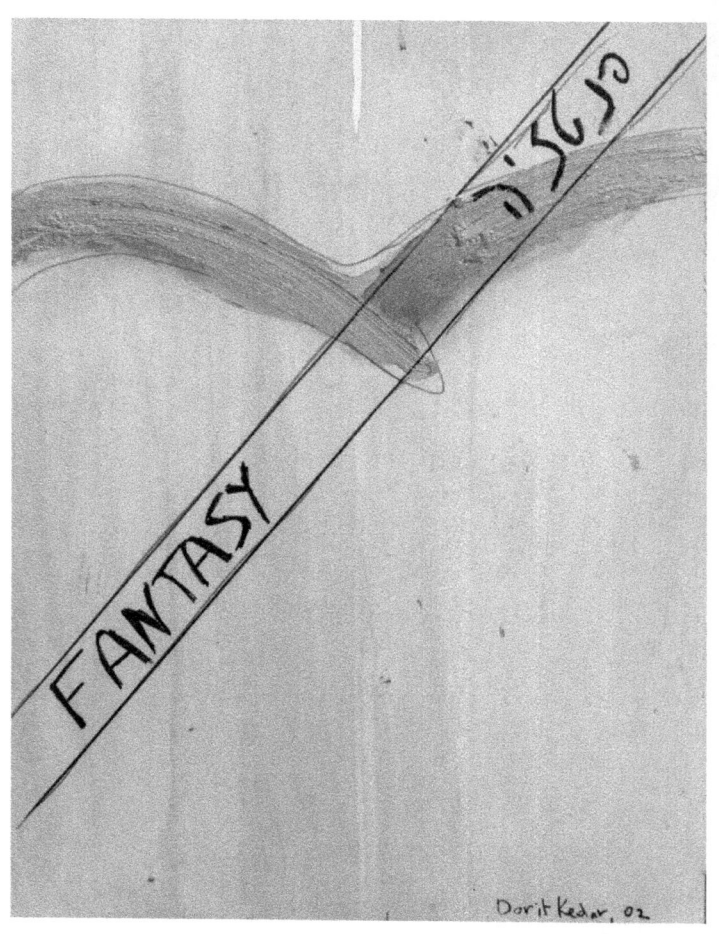

Cab Story ∗ *Dorit Kedar*

From Ramat Ha'Chaiil to "Yefet" Gallery in Jaffa

DRIVER: Oh, it's you. I'm sorry you had to wait, I was on Oley Ha'Gardom and not Harugey Ha'Malchut.*
*(street names that relate to a group of executed individuals)

THE PASSENGER: No, you were on Harugey Ha'Malchut instead of being on Oley Ha'Gardom.

DRIVER: Boy, what's going with me, being confused this way and especially with you. You're like my sister, you have a good heart I love. Do you know Gato? I call him Gatuta. *[to the radio]* Gatuta, you hear? Who do I have here? Guess! Maybe we can ask her to go fishing on Saturday morning on the yacht. Yes, she says she'll go, gladly, she says.

THE PASSENGER: What's wrong with you? I did not say yes. I hate fishing, I don't eat fish. I don't eat any animal, for that matter.

DRIVER: Gatuta, I went to Abas, the fishnet guy. What can I tell you? There's so many fish in the ocean! No, don't say anything, don't jinx it! You brought your wife some of the catch? Probably turned them into delicacies, but don't say anything! Don't jinx it! So we're taking Dorit out on Saturday, whatever she wants us to do, we will!

THE PASSENGER: Uri, I already told you, I don't eat fish and I certainly don't get up early on Saturday mornings.

DRIVER: Don't have a fit, no yacht, no fish. But it's a secret. All the cabbies go wild; they want to go on the yacht. We even showed them a picture of a yacht and they think it's for real, the fools. I was accidently born a cab driver, actually I'm an actor, would love to do a bit in the theater. You just ask Uri and Gatuta onto the stage, we go up there, both of us the same height, looking at each other and the crowd would go wild.

Do me a favor, Dorit, pleeeeeease, call Connie the dispatcher and tell him you want Uri for a thing in the theater. He'll have a fit. He's a good guy, but he's like an ad in the paper. Tell him something and everyone's gonna know about it. Don't forget. No, don't call him from the cab, call from home, so he wouldn't suspect something's up.

THE PASSENGER: In this heat you had me running all the way from Oley Ha'Gardom and they already told you I was there and still nothing. You always do this, every time, and this time I have an important meeting. Can't you guys tell the difference? Why should you? The dead here, the dead there, it's all the same to you.

DRIVER: A thousand apologizes, a thousand.

THE PASSENGER: Tell that dispatcher that you made a mistake. I was driving them crazy over there. He of course said you were down in the street already, only it was a different street, right? Ahh, this heat!

DRIVER: You're putting on make up?

THE PASSENGER: Of course, after I dried up and my face was melting.

DRIVER: You sure are a pretty woman.

THE PASSENGER: Thank you…

DRIVER: But I'm not into women, myself.

THE PASSENGER: You're into fish!

DRIVER: Good for you…

THE PASSENGER: You're not into men?!

DRIVER: No, I'm into you!

THE PASSENGER: Me? How about that? You really shouldn't be, I'm far from the ideal woman type.

DRIVER: I can see that.

THE PASSENGER: What do you mean you can "see that?"

DRIVER: I can see you're not ideal just as I can see you're pretty. But I'm far from ideal myself. Well, can I go with you?

THE PASSENGER: And what are we to do together? Will you go to the opera?

DRIVER: Yeah, I'm a musician and a masseuse as well. I took classes in Thailand for years and I can work each nook in your body. So, what do you say? You have someone? I'll give you my card, you'll be sorry if you don't take it!

THE PASSENGER: This cab pulled up with three men inside–I didn't get in!

DRIVER: Three men and you didn't get on? Lucky you! Life's a ball. I adore women. They do it to me. I only hope that when I'm 80, they'll still do it to me, but who am I gonna do at 80? A 70-year-old woman? Not on your life! Women at that age just give up, they don't give it up.

THE PASSENGER: So you're in constant need of women?

DRIVER: Yeah, why not? You pull over, have a little fun.

THE PASSENGER: And your wife?

DRIVER: She's no problem. I'm a good husband. Don't drink, don't play the cards, a good provider!

THE PASSENGER: Very good, but you can be a good provider, not drink, not play cards and not run around. So? Do that many women succumb to you that you pull over and go up to have a little fun?

DRIVER: Frankly? No.

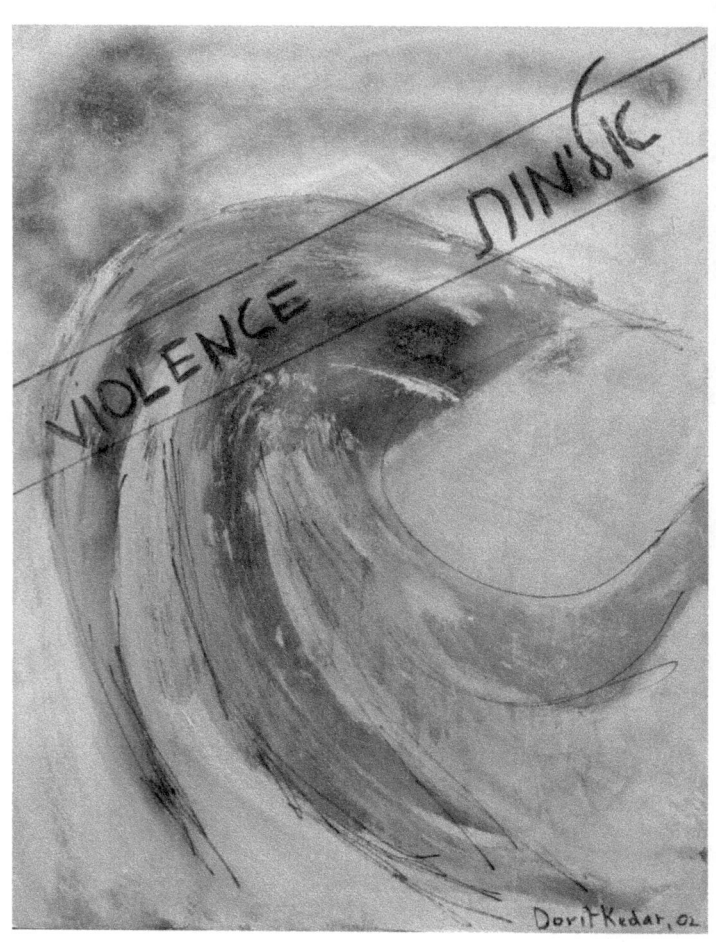

Cab Story * Dorit Kedar

From Ramat Ha'Chaiil to the Mediation Section at the Department of Justice

THE PASSENGER: Bon appetite. The carrot, I mean.

DRIVER: Thanks.

THE PASSENGER: It's good that I see you with that carrot. I should go on a diet. These holiday pastries have cost me a pound or two. I should go on Ramadan.

DRIVER: Just keep it shut! No eating, at all. Da wife's that way, never eats. If you see her after 3 babies, she's a looker. But me, I love to eat. Love to have it all. Lately I've been off red meat, but I used to have a lot.

THE PASSENGER: So maybe you should refine yourself a little. Avid meat eaters are prone to violence.

DRIVER: I ain't violent!

THE PASSENGER: You're not?

DRIVER: Nah! I just adjust to da environment. I live in Rishon.

THE PASSENGER: Nice place.

DRIVER: Nice place, shitty people.

THE PASSENGER: Is that a characteristic of Rishon, "Shitty population?"

DRIVER: No, people are shitty everywhere. But it's okay, I guess, a nice place.

THE PASSENGER: So, under what circumstances are you violent?

DRIVER: Only when they really tick me off! I'll give you one—I hate it when someone takes my parking.

THE PASSENGER: Is it yours? Did you buy it?

*Cab Story * Dorit Kedar*

DRIVER: Yeah, paid good money for it, too. I come home one day to park, and I find this car on my spot. I parked da car on da side like that, so no one can get out, like in a prison, yeah, until they found da guy and it turned out he was visiting one of da tenants. I din't mind so much but all da others were screaming their heads off, so today everyone knows not to mess with my spot. Another one? Look, I live on da 4th floor. On da 5th there's this family that keeps shaking their carpets on everybody's heads, and no one says nothin'. I went upstairs, talked with that woman, talked to her husband, again with da wife. Nothing helps. Then at da tenants meeting I started up with'em, called her a piece of shit and all. Da husband said he'd have a piece of me, so I asked him: "you wanna go at it before or after you're dead?" Then it got really loud and da cops came over. I told da cop about da carpets and told him I was willing to go get a whiskey bottle as a peace offering to that piece of shit from up stairs, that came from da Tikva neighborhood and were used to living on da ground floor and shake

their carpets on da ground. Then da
cop warned me not to go upstairs.
Today it's all good. I help him change
his tires, fix his car when he needs it
and they help me and it's all good.
This traffic! I'll give you another one:
above us there's this couple, think
their home is a soccer stadium or
somethin'. I sit in my living room and
go crazy. I went to see da wife, da
husband, da big brother. Nothing
helps. Then, like I told you, I'm in my
living room and it's all bang-bang
upstairs. I ran up there. Da wife
wanted to slam da door in my face, so
I shoved it back and her husband din't
even budge. Good thing he din't
either, smart move. Today it's like that
floor was blown off da earth, can't
hear a thing, d'you catch my drift? And
I ain't violent, I'm in control. I just
react and fit to my environment.
Where did you want to? No, no, I'll
take you all da way up there, so it'll
be easier on you.

Cab Story * *Dorit Kedar*

From Ramat Ha'Chaiil to "Yefet" Gallery in Jaffa

THE PASSENGER: Please turn down both radios. Don't worry, here, I am making it up to you with some gum and cherry-mint candy.

DRIVER: Then it's all worth it! I can't do without the radio, it's on 24/7. If the wife or the kids turn it off, I wake up immediately. "But you were sleeping," says the wife. Nothing, without some noise in the background I can't sleep. Even when I close my eyes I can hear "goal!"

THE PASSENGER: Into soccer, are you?

DRIVER: Very much, but I haven't been going to the stadiums for 15 years now. Have you ever been to a soccer match?

THE PASSENGER: No, but I've seen one on TV.

DRIVER: It's not the real deal. Only in this country they have these high bars that separate the team from the spectators, like animals. They don't have that in Europe. UEFA wants them out, but here we need bars. The spectators, and I mean all of them–cabbies, those lawyers and those people who run the banks–all of them curse and scream and after the game go home and won't even dream about repeating those kind of words again, even alone, under the shower. It's all these wars we have here, made us violent. I'm in a parachutes brigade on reserve duty. You should see those big-shot lawyers and bank people eating with their hands like animals, and dripping all over the place, and that's what's so special about it. But classical music, the kind with violins–I like on real low, and I hate honking, too. Why do they honk so much in Israel? To get a friend's attention on the other side of the street. You're rushing off to work?

THE PASSENGER: Yes, work, work, haven't won the lottery yet.

*Cab Story * Dorit Kedar*

DRIVER: Do you play it?

THE PASSENGER: Maybe won 10, 100 shekels in the past ten years playing the same numbers every time.

DRIVER: Bad luck you have there.

THE PASSENGER: And you?

DRIVER: Me, too, but I know people with good luck, like this friend of mine who's won, twice and big! But when it's bad luck, it's bad luck all the way!

THE PASSENGER: Maybe we should play together, you and I?

DRIVER: No way. Two wrongs don't make a right. Nothing helps. Let me tell you something, if a friend of yours plays your numbers, he'll take it! And if it was the other way around, no go. Bad luck is bad luck all the way. So long!

*Cab Story * Dorit Kedar*

From Ramat Ha'Chaiil to the Tel Aviv Museum of Art

THE PASSENGER: That dreadful group rape with the four men and one girl is a catastrophe.

DRIVER: They should cut it off like they do thieves with their hands, but what went on there?

THE PASSENGER: Four guys abducted a girl, pulled over, bought some alcohol, got some drugs and raped her one after the other.

DRIVER: So they were high?

THE PASSENGER: Yes.

DRIVER: Then it's not a rape.

THE PASSENGER: Isn't it?

DRIVER: They were high, you say!

THE PASSENGER: Turn down that radio, that techno music is too loud.

DRIVER: A headache?

THE PASSENGER: No, I just don't care much for noise. But I'm getting off soon, don't worry.

DRIVER: I have to have the radio on not to fall asleep, I work all night. At night's better, quieter, but boring. *[noise from the car radio]* That was my son on the radio, I got one for him and for my daughter, expensive ones, each one over 2,000 shekels.

THE PASSENGER: Radios instead of visiting? You must be divorced.

DRIVER: Yes, I am, and I really can't find the time to go and visit them. I spend most of my time by myself, but I talk to them on the radio.

THE PASSENGER: You do realize that is no substitute, no reason, and that if you don't put in the effort now, you'll lose.

DRIVER: Since my mother's passed away I haven't seen much of them. She was like a wife to me, cooked, did the laundry, the kids were always over at her house.

THE PASSENGER: But you're the children's father, you should be there for them like your mother was for you. You have to get past being a son in order to become a father.

DRIVER: They really do ask me to come over a lot. Maybe I can come to you for counseling?

THE PASSENGER: I already gave you free advice.

DRIVER: Would you like my card so you could call me for rides?

THE PASSENGER: No, thank you, I already have someone.

DRIVER: So? One more to bug you.

THE PASSENGER: No, why do you say bug. Hand the card over, one can never know.

DRIVER: You can call me for other reasons, too.

THE PASSENGER: Like for what? Like a call girl?

DRIVER: No, sister, you won't make it as a call girl. Maybe you have a PhD in something, but a call girl can get one, too.

THE PASSENGER: But you just asked me to call you.

DRIVER: Listen, it's a pity you're getting off, otherwise I would have explained to you what's a call-girl-PhD and how you'd never get one.

Cab Story * Dorit Kedar

From Ramat Ha'Chaiil to the "Simta" Theater

THE PASSENGER: Hello, is that you I called?

DRIVER: Yes, it's me, Herzl, like the visionary of the state, best number to call at the station.

THE PASSENGER: So you're feeling well?

DRIVER: Very. Curses on all my enemies.

THE PASSENGER: Have you many?

DRIVER: Do I... But it won't help them, I have providence. I almost died 3 times and I am still alive. When I last came back from the US (I have a lot going on, curses on all my enemies), I got that flesh-eating bacteria. I stayed at the hospital unconscious for a month and came out all because my ancestors were looking down upon me.

My rabbi said it was my grandfather, may he rest in peace. I said Kadish for a whole year on his behalf. The second time was during the Golf War. I was working for a newspaper every night. One day I'm in my bed and an angel in a white robe, long white beard and this cap that looked like Little Red Riding Hood's on its head said, "arise, arise, leave your home." And I didn't want to, but the angel insisted, "arise, get out of your home." And so I did and after I did, bang! The missile hit our house on the spot!

THE PASSENGER: And the third time?

DRIVER: I was on a red light and this girl came up behind me doing 90 inside the city, totaled the whole car, lost her legs and all and me, I got the traffic light pole stuck in my throat, my legs got broken and my head split open. That's how it is, they don't get on the wheel to go on a joyride, they go out to war, dickheads!*

THE PASSENGER: What's a "dickhead?"

DRIVER: What? You're not native? "dickhead" means jerk.

THE PASSENGER: I was actually born here, and you?

DRIVER: I came here when I was 6, so, what does that make me?

THE PASSENGER: Sweetheart, it makes you a dickhead.

---

* In the original appears a derogatory term derived from Iraqi Arabic. The driver asks the passenger if she is an Ashkenazi (as in Ashkenazi Jew, originating from Europe mainly, unlike a Sephardic Jew, who originated from countries in Northern Africa or the Arabian Peninsula), denoting derision. He also says he came from an area at the Iranian-Russian border.

*Cab Story * Dorit Kedar*

From Old Jaffa to Ramat Ha'Chaiil

THE PASSENGER: I visited this old man, rich, sick and childless.

DRIVER: And you visit him–why?

THE PASSENGER: I try to, yes. All the other rich people deserted him and besides, he is not a very nice man. Today he had to say that I am wearing too many stripes, have too many chains around my neck, a spare one on my eyeglasses, rows of white hairs on my head and split teeth. But that mean old man–I just don't respond.

DRIVER: Squeeze some money out of him. He doesn't have anyone else to give it to, so he can give it to you. He probably has some around the house. Rip him off.

THE PASSENGER: He has it at the bank.

DRIVER: So tell him it's for burial procedures, headstone, marble, things like that.

THE PASSENGER: No, I think I'll just keep visiting him.

DRIVER: The love of men, you say, huh? I'm an Arab and for me, we are all the same, even the gays. The Arabs want to kill all gays, such stupidity. I look at them on Gay Pride day, they look like women. It's the hormones, they're not to blame. Lesbians, neither. I had a thing with a lesbian once, didn't want me to touch her or feel her up. Nothing, nothing at all, just wanted to give head.

THE PASSENGER: Then she wasn't a lesbian! What is your name? Na'aman…? Na'aman!

DRIVER: Maybe not a lesbian, but a cocksucker and I never done such a thing, but I must say I enjoyed it. She was a pro! Could hardly feel her teeth.

THE PASSENGER: So what happened?

DRIVER: I went a couple of times to see her, and that's it. I'm married and have a beautiful wife, grandchildren, and girlfriends.

THE PASSENGER: Girlfriends, too? When do you see these girlfriends?

DRIVER: Whenever I want. How did we end up on this subject?

Cab Story ∗ Dorit Kedar

From Ramat Ha'Chaiil to Beit Berl

DRIVER: Hello! What about the cab stories book? Let me tell you one. One night this beautiful young lady gets into my cab, stinks of alcohol, gets close to me and asks, "driver, wanna have some fun?" I told her, "toots, I'm a married man, but I know this single guy who might be into it." What a looker, such a looker. I got on the radio and asked my single buddy if he wanted to come down to the station, because I have a surprise for him, a gift, so he came over, picked her up, she blew his mind and then he told us over the radio that she had another six that night.

THE PASSENGER: A very prolific evening.

DRIVER: No, she wasn't a hooker.

THE PASSENGER: So?

DRIVER: For the heck of it. She loves it. Since that night, she disappeared off the face of the earth, no one knows where she is, vanished. And that's not all, one time I'm driving along and this totally naked chick gets in my car. I asked her, "where will you pull the fare from?" and believe you me, she had it and she didn't go that far, either. Well, it was very nice, see you, hope you enjoyed the stories.

Epilogue

THE PASSENGER: Hijo! What's up?

DRIVER: Did you call my nurse girlfriend, Dorit, like I asked you to?

THE PASSENGER: Sure I did, and not once. I explained to her that I'm a good client of yours and that I feel bad for you. I told her of course that you are also very sorry, that you won't act like a total fool and that you are begging for her to come back. She of course does not believe you. It took me several calls to persuade her that you transformed yourself, seriously this time. Hijo, I hope this time you'll really act like a civilized man.

About the author

Israeli born Dorit Kedar is an artist, theorist, art critic and curator. She holds degrees in translation, comparative literature, philosophy, eastern philosophy, art history and obtained her PhD in Creative Arts from Union College, Cincinnati.

She currently teaches art history and eastern philosophy at the "Midrasha" – Faculty of the Arts at Beit Berl Academic College, Israel.

She is the founder and head of the Center of Inter-religious Peace in Tel Aviv.

Digital version of this publication available as well
Original Hebrew version available for download
Paintings available for purchase

More titles by the author in Hebrew and English:

The Book of Inter-religious Peace in Word and Image

Caravaggio as a Modernist: What is Modernism?

Tarot and Zen Buddhism: A Gradual Way to Increase the Consciousness of Inclusion

http://doritkedar.wordpress.com/store/

www.ingramcontent.com/pod-product-compliance
Lightning Source LLC
Chambersburg PA
CBHW071743040426
42446CB00012B/2449